I'VE GOT YOUR NUMBER

I've Got Your Number!

A BOOK OF SELF-ANALYSIS

by

DORIS WEBSTER

&

MARY ALDEN HOPKINS

APPLEWOOD BOOKS

Carlisle, Massachusetts

978-1-4290-9671-3

MANUFACTURED IN THE UNITED STATES OF AMERICA
WITH AMERICAN-MADE MATERIALS

I've Got Your Number!

I'VE GOT YOUR NUMBER

YOUR response to these questions gives the key to your character.

DIRECTIONS (READ CAREFULLY)

Read each of the following questions carefully and after impartial consideration answer each one "yes" or "no."

Do not omit any answer, as omission is construed as a negative answer.

If you feel that you cannot answer definitely "yes" or "no," remember that the situation described should be considered in its usual aspect, without addition of extraordinary circumstances. For example, if the question is, "Would you walk five blocks to see a parade?" do not assume, on the one hand, that you might have sprained your ankle, nor, on the other, that the president of the United States might be marching in the parade.

Answer as fairly as you can what would be your normal reaction under normal conditions.

If you still feel that your answer cannot be a positive "yes" or "no," give whichever answer seems to have the balance of weight on its side. In such questions as, "Do people come to you for advice?" compare yourself with the *average* man or woman, to the best of your ability, and answer accordingly.

To find your key:

Each of the questions in the five groups, including five questions each, must be answered. If your answer is "yes" to three or more of the questions under Group 1, your key number begins with the digit "1." If it is "no," omit "1" from your key number. In the same way, if you answer most of the questions in Group 2 in the affirmative, the number "2" is a digit in your key number; if most of these questions are answered in the negative, "2" is omitted, and so on with each group.

For example, suppose you answer "yes" to the majority of the questions in Group 2, Group 4, and Group 5, and "no" to the majority in Groups 1 and 3, your key number will be 245.

To take other examples, if you answer "yes" to the majority of questions in every group, your key number will be 12345; if "no," it will be 0. If you answer "no" to the majority of questions in each of the first four groups and "yes" to the majority in the last group, your key number will be 5.

When you have ascertained your key number, look it up on page 16 if you are a man or 94 if you are a woman, and you will find your analysis.

EXAMPLE

Group 1		Group 2		Group 3		Group 4		Group 5	
A	*Yes*	A	*No*	A	*Yes*	A	*Yes*	A	*Yes*
B	*No*	B	*Yes*	B	*Yes*	B	*Yes*	B	*Yes*
C	*No*	C	*Yes*	C	*No*	C	*Yes*	C	*No*
D	*No*	D	*Yes*	D	*No*	D	*Yes*	D	*Yes*
E	*Yes*	E	*No*	E	*No*	E	*Yes*	E	*No*

No		*Yes*		*No*		*Yes*		*Yes*	
—		2		—		4		5	

Key number = 245

QUESTIONS FOR MEN

For directions see page 1

GROUP 1

A—Do you wake up despondent?

B—Do most of the people on the street look dissatisfied?

C—Have you been unlucky in your business relations?

D—Can you hold a grievance three years?

E—Do you think people talk against you behind your back?

GROUP 2

A—Do you prefer to make decisions rather than to let circumstances decide for you?

B—Is success usually the result of honest effort?

C—Do people come to you for advice?

D—Are your mistakes your own fault?

E—Do you get your own way?

GROUP 3

A—Have you definitely planned your career five years ahead?

B—Did you choose your profession or business yourself?

C—Would you accept promotion if it meant much increased work or responsibility?

D—Is a husband's primary duty to be a good provider?

E—Would you rather start your own business than invest in an established enterprise?

GROUP 4

A—Are your day-dreams impractical?

B—Do you put off till to-morrow what you should do to-day?

C—Do you like to be alone with your thoughts?

D—Do people nag you?

E—Are you a fitful worker?

GROUP 5

A—Do you think the average woman is out for all she can get?

B—Do you think early marriage undesirable?

C—Do women shirk?

D—Would you prefer belonging to a club of men only rather than to a club of men and women?

E—When poverty comes in at the door does love fly out of the window?

KEY NUMBERS FOR MEN

CHARACTER STUDIES FOR MEN

Key Number 0

HOW easily you adjust yourself to any situation! No one knows better than you how to get along with this world, avoiding all unnecessary difficulties, going about your own business, and having a good time while you do it.

If you really want to hear your faults—which you probably do not, for you have no passion for criticism—it might be mentioned that you rather side-step an embarrassing situation if you can; not that you shirk, for you certainly do your share of the world's work, but you do not always grasp the nettle and pull it up. It would not do, however, for you to try to change yourself in this respect, for in the first place you could not, and in the second place most of the people around you would be sorry to see you any different. And, as a matter of fact, you usually get rid of the nettle somehow even if you do not use extreme measures. You are not at all the kind to suffer in silence.

You are ideal in the home, for you take a great interest in it; and ideal in the office, where your work is excellent and where your tact keeps things running smoothly. Although you are not worldly, you might make a good deal of money. You get along with most women so well that you might make the mistake of choosing a sickly tyrant.

Key Number 1

LIFE to you is pretty much one task after another. Although you keep everlastingly at it, your work never grows less, and you get discouraged because you see no let-up ahead of you. You often tell your wife, or maybe it is your mother or your sweetheart, or even a pleasant strange woman whom you meet on the train by chance, that sometimes you are ready to end it all. You never say this to a man for fear he will laugh at you, but women are always kind to you; that is, almost always. Sometimes they get impatient with you because you do not make the most of yourself.

Try to see your life, past, present, and future, like a picture. The past will be very clear, the present should be definite and concrete, while the future will be necessarily a little vague. Nevertheless the future should show bold outlines, which can be altered if necessary. You should have a fairly well formulated idea of what you are going to do and how you are going to do it. As you go ahead with your work you will change your plans more or less to fit into circumstances. Keep details subordinated to your general scheme, putting your mind on them as they come up one by one.

Your greatest asset is a characteristic which may easily become a hindrance if not held in check. You are prone to be contented. This is excellent when applied to your wife and children and house and cigars. But you must not be content with your own achievements to the extent of ceasing your exertions.

Key Number 2

UNLESS you are still very young, you are on various committees and are having difficulty keeping yourself off of others. You are the kind that people turn to for organizing work, first because you do it well, and second because you are willing to take the time from your own affairs in order to get an organization working. You take satisfaction in seeing that it does work, yet you do not insist on bossing the whole show. You are a good executive, especially when it is a matter of managing something not connected with your own business.

You would make an excellent husband, and you would have sense enough to choose a wife wisely and not be carried away by mere youth and beauty. You are fond of children, extremely fond of your home, and would probably like to garden. You like social life for its friendliness but are rather bored by "high life." It doesn't seem to you worth bothering about. You would rather have a good cook than a good butler. You like camping trips, dogs, the theater, and the sea. You would likely be intrigued by a ship model and would like to make one yourself. While you are not looking for trouble, you do not let people impose on you. The woman who marries you is lucky.

Key Number 3

WOMEN like you, and you like women. You have pleasant little ways of helping with the dishes and lugging heavy chairs which endear a guest to a hostess more than the parlor tricks with banjo and cards. A party always "goes" when you are there. What's more, your own women-folks who see you every day all the year are as fond of you as outsiders are, and that is more than many a man can say. Though they prod you, it is for your own good, as they often tell you. The actual reason that you flare up or gloom when they get after you is because your conscience tells you that they are right and that you shouldn't have—well, we'll say no more, for you get the idea.

Once upon a time there was a man who had all the virtues, and several of the vices also. Now, this isn't you, but maybe you will be interested to hear how he treated his tendency to take one more drink. Or maybe it was his habit of playing poker for high stakes. Or maybe it was his exceeding interest in girls he wasn't really interested in at all. He made up in his mind a picture of what he actually wanted in life: high standing among his fellow-men, a moderate income, a good house, a contented wife, two well brought up children. Every night he went to sleep picturing this desire to himself. Soon he began planning how to get these things. Gradually his attention shifted from his old not wholly satisfactory activities and centered itself on attaining the satisfactions he really wanted. In the end he had everything he had listed, a lot more, and had enjoyed the struggle to make good.

Key Number 4

YOU have worked out your own philosophy of life, and it is an excellent one—for you. But not for most men, for not many have your buoyancy, sense of humor, and ability to get a great deal of satisfaction out of little things. You can get just as much pleasure out of a shack as another man gets out of a palace; probably more.

While in some cases it is better for a man to marry his opposite, you would probably do well to choose some one whose outlook on life is rather like your own. She might well have more energy, but if she yearned too much for Rolls-Royces and pearls your marriage might go on the rocks. That would be a pity, for with the right wife you could be ideally happy.

Your personality is intriguing, and it is hard to do it justice. You are friendly toward the world, just and loving. Children amuse you, and you like to give them little presents. You like to watch young animals play. You probably like to smoke, and you would like to fish except that you have notions that the fish do not enjoy it. You are not interested in shooting. You like yourself, and can amuse yourself with your own fancies.

With the wrong environment your rare nature might be harmed, but fortunately you have the habit of getting away from the wrong environment. You do not fight the things that you don't like, but you leave them alone. If there were more like you, the world might not move so fast, but it would be a happier place.

Key Number 5

You have wonderful ability in making the best of things. Maybe you would be better off if you weren't so pleasant and kind and, might one say, easy-going. Can you not remember many occasions when you got into trouble and got other people into trouble also because you took the easiest way out of a difficult situation?

You do hate a row, and you will do anything to avoid one. Can you not learn that sometimes the best, easiest, and kindest method of dealing with persons who are in the wrong is to blow them up good and hard once and for all? You are the type of man who is likely to be imposed on by others. This sort of man is a temptation to other people because he is so obliging about doing work which they should attend to themselves. Deep in his heart he knows that something is being put over on him, and after a while he becomes resentful. Resentment is a slow-burning anger which never did anybody any good. So the thing for you to do is to carry your own burdens with the bravery you have always shown but not take on extra loads which other people should lug themselves.

All of the energy which has been escaping through doing things which are pleasant but harmful should be turned into driving yourself forward toward the goal which you have chosen. If you have not chosen a goal, turn your attention to that matter immediately.

Key Number 12

YOU have one trait that holds you back—unevenness of temperament. That may be due to your early training, or possibly to ill health, but whatever the cause you should overcome it if possible. Of course, you have no special reason for trying to fight your disquieting moods, for you are not particularly anxious to make a spectacular success, but it seems a pity that your really fine qualities should sometimes be overshadowed by your tendency toward trivial complaints.

When you are feeling your best you are a joy to all about you, actively interested in others, and ready to help with their immediate problems. It is only when you are in one of your "Oh, what's the use!" moods that you are something of a trial.

You are liberal, logical, and willing to concede women their due—a priceless quality. Why do you have periods of ill feeling? It is not exactly because of envy, for in your heart you do not covet your neighbor's chauffeur. You really don't care for money very much, yet you are rather indignant when the other fellow has it, especially if he has inherited it.

It might be a good idea if you studied yourself, formulated a philosophy, and remembered it. You have the strength deliberately to remake yourself if you want to, and you are too fine to let yourself run to seed.

Key Number 13

YOU wonder more frequently than do most people what life is all about anyhow; where we came from, where we are going, where we are now, and if it is really worth while hanging round to find out. When you were a child this characteristic was called "glumness," but you prefer to think of it as despondency; if your wife is a wise woman she will accept the characteristic as "going into the silence" and not fuss about it. Maybe she will be smart enough to say: "He has the artist's temperament! The poor dear really should have been a poet!"

Suddenly up from the depths you rise on wings of hope, and, hurrah, it's a fine old world after all! Life is one grand sweet song in your heart. You become the I-can man. You pick up the tasks that have been dragging and send them spinning along toward their goal. You work in a frenzy of energy, and your co-workers seem slow and lazy. You tell your wife, or will when you get one, about the house she is going to have, and together you look over motor-car advertisements. Thanks to these bursts of energy, you keep your job, and progress, but much more slowly than you would if you could hold a steadier gait. Thanks to these spells of delight in life, your wife still loves you, although you demand a deal of patience.

The curious part of it is that your friends have little knowledge of all this tumultuous inner life of yours, for on the surface you seem very much like the other fellows in your set. In the hidden depths of your soul you are unique.

Key Number 14

YOU would like to sit by the fire, wearing an old smoking-jacket and holding the cat. But you would not necessarily be thinking placid thoughts. You are inclined to be introspective and spend considerable time thinking about yourself. But that does not mean that you are selfish. You would forget to feed yourself before you would forget to feed your dog.

You are the kind who gets along very well with a wife, and you are really much happier than you think you are, especially as you secretly believe that some day you are going to startle the world by achieving a great success.

You are a little inclined to carp at other people's suggestions, just for the pleasure of carping, but you are not really hard to get along with, because you are fundamentally reasonable.

Your kindness is perhaps your most lovable characteristic, and your straightforwardness your most admirable. You detest a "smart Aleck" and other forms of cheapness. If some little thing goes wrong, particularly if it means that your feelings are hurt, it may spoil your whole day and color your philosophy ultramarine; but normally your outlook on life is friendly and your attitude toward others free from cynicism.

Key Number 15

YOU have the delightful quality of enjoying your friends, admiring your possessions, fitting your job, and cherishing your intimates. You do not in your heart consider millions worth the effort Rockefeller and Ford had to make to get their money. Oh, you'd take a hundred thousand with thanks if it were just around the corner, but you would not dig to the depths of the earth for it, nor raise great factories, nor direct the activities of ten thousand men, for the sake of making money. You are a steady, conscientious worker, but not an adventurer.

This lack of longing to make yourself miserable doing what you don't want to do, for the sake of something you may never get, sometimes gives you a guilty feeling. Occasionally you feel out of harmony with this world of go-getters. Other people think you are having a grouch, and you yourself are not quite sure what is the trouble. You wonder if you ought to see a doctor, but just then some extra work comes up or the rain stops or you meet a new girl, and you are comfortable again.

I'VE GOT YOUR NUMBER

Girls, wives, aunts, female cousins, and even your mother are continual disappointments to you. Woman, lovely woman, is not, you find, the ministering angel she has been called. You are polite about it—usually—but you do not really think much of women. Your type is likely to remain unmarried, or if married to find it difficult to make sufficient concessions to insure a happy marriage. You expect too much of women, and unless you learn to take them as they are, they will bring you only disappointment and suffering.

Key Number 23

YOU are impeccable! Your only fault is that you are faultless. You are the kind of man whom parents pick out for a girl to marry—and afterward they are able to say that they were right too. You are really kind, not merely lavish, to women; you keep your temper and stick to your job instead of wasting time in idle complaints; you have a sense of humor and can even laugh at yourself sometimes; you are a good workman, a firm but just business man, and would make an excellent husband and a loving father. Not another one of the men analyzed in these pages has the number of good traits that you have.

You see things in their right relationship and can appreciate the other man's point of view and do not feed your vanity by disparaging others. You are the type that is voted the "most popular man" in school or college.

The best of it is that instead of being smugly pleased with the above analysis you are wondering if there isn't something wrong with you just because there is nothing about you to criticize. Don't worry about that; you're all right. Ask the Chamber of Commerce. Ask the men at the club. Ask the girls. Ask mother—she knows!

Key Number 24

YOU do not have to wait till you are dead to have people speak well of you. Sometimes you are ashamed because you think you do not deserve the affection that is showered upon you and the praises that are chorused behind your back. Don't worry; you have your critics, too, who underestimate you as others overestimate you.

You will never be wholly content with yourself, because you will never reach your goal. The reason for this is somewhat peculiar. As you approach your goal, you are looking forward to one further distant and pass your original one without noticing it. Before you finish one achievement, you are already started on the next, although you always complete what you begin.

If you have employees, they like to work for you, and while you are still young they begin referring to you kindly as "the old man," for you are the sort on whom others instinctively lean and to whom they turn for direction and advice. Your wife is—or will be, if you have not yet married—a fortunate woman and knows it. In fact other women feel she is a bit smug about her husband. The worst criticism brought against you is that you are impractical. The finest that is said of you is that you never let anybody down.

Key Number 25

YOU'VE got to be very careful about choosing your wife! Oh, yes, you can get along with most women, and you think one is as good as another; but that's just the trouble. You think of women collectively. You bunch them all together, and you say somewhat cynically, "They're all alike." Some day you may wake up and find out that they aren't. Do make a special study of them before it is too late, with reference not to the color of their eyes and hair (about which you know plenty already) but to their honesty, courage, and brains and unselfishness and similar essentials.

This point must be emphasized, for otherwise there is little to warn you against. You are a good all-round man, popular with men, willing to do your share of unpleasant work, and delightfully sunny by nature. People probably talk about that nice smile of yours.

You like the theater—if it isn't too highbrow—the movies, tennis, and other sports and fishing. You are interested in politics and would enjoy travel. You ought to have a happy life ahead of you if you will get over that slightly cynical attitude toward women. For when you disparage women you are unconsciously laying up trouble for yourself.

Key Number 34

ONCE there was a man who day-dreamed about a boiling tea-kettle, and as a result we have the steamboat. Other men have made their fancies into poems, novels, paintings, and beautiful buildings. You have this same tendency to wander off into an imaginary world, but you have not yet learned that it may be an element of strength instead of a weakness. Nobody but yourself knows how you long to be a success. In fact you will very likely flatly contradict this statement. That is because you do not yet see your way ahead very clearly.

The next time you have a spare hour and there is no one around to jeer at you, write down on a slip of paper all the things you want to do, the positions you want to hold, and the triumphs you wish to accomplish. Draw a line through those that are obviously impossible. From those that are left choose the one that is dearest to you. From now on concentrate on how you can bring to pass what you most desire.

I'VE GOT YOUR NUMBER

Your optimism in the face of difficulties and your friendliness are among your best assets. Talk it all over with the One Possible She and ask her what she thinks about it.

Key Number 35

WERE you tied to some one's apron-strings too long? Your chief trouble seems to be that you lack self-confidence, for otherwise you are an excellent all-round type. Think over that apron-string matter, however, for it may have rather warped you in several different respects. For one thing, you may still resent the influence that kept you from freely following your own bent when you were younger, and you may have transferred that resentment to other people —whole groups of people. You want to be careful not to hold a subconsciously hostile attitude toward your wife. If you feel irritated when she wants you to polish your shoes, remember that there is nothing at all in that suggestion that ought to make you angry. Your anger is a hang-over from some early resentment.

In more important matters, however, you may give in too easily, but that is because you do not trust your own judgment. Try to be firm where you can dispassionately justify your firmness; and when you yield,

yield without rancor. You should be able to do this, for you have naturally a sunny disposition.

You would probably get along best with a woman who was very much interested in her own affairs, for if she were chiefly interested in yours you would ask her advice one day and resent her interference the next. Get acquainted with many women before you marry. In most respects you should find life easy; your big problem will be your marriage.

Key Number 45

YOU are on rather good terms with life and forgive it the hard blows which it has dealt you. You get more biffs than most men because of your blithe manner of walking straight up to trouble. But you have never learned to cross to the opposite sidewalk when you see temptation coming down the street—even though you know you will wake up with a headache next morning. It doesn't do any good to try to lecture you about doing the things you should not do and leaving undone the things you should do, because you are the only person who can change your personality, and you haven't yet taken the trouble to do so. You answer all criticism with a pleasant smile and agree that the speaker is right.

It is rather a pity that you do not get busy being in reality as efficient as you might be, but so far you have found it too much effort. You have such fine qualities of gaiety, good humor, and light-heartedness. There seems to be no jealousy, envy, rancor, or other mean quality in you. You can get on with almost any man you ever meet. You are not so fortunate with women, but this is because women have a tendency to scold you about your failings. Like most men, you identify your women-folk with your conscience, and both of them speak harsh words to you all too often. So long as you are on bad terms with your conscience—as you are, you know—you will not be comfortable with women. You would better make terms with both of them if you wish to be fully at ease in the world.

Key Number 123

YOU like a thunder-storm, the more thundery the better. You would like to be a part of it; you feel almost as if you were.

It is hard to criticize your type, for your faults are romantic ones, and women love you for them and would not like to see you reform. They like you, too, for your protective ways and the strength which your personality suggests.

You are not a poseur at all, for you are too much interested in what you are doing to think about how you appear to others. You have a strong interest in poetry and art, and it is a sincere one. But you also like practical matters, and business interests you. You would be at your best if you were in some active business that had an artistic or romantic side. In the old days you might have been captain of a whaling ship.

Sensible women like you as much as the flappers do, for you are able to take an interest in them as human beings without always thinking of them as women.

To some extent you consider the world your oyster —and perhaps it is. You are one of the lucky ones in life, deny it though you will.

Key Number 124

FREQUENTLY your wife, or maybe it is your mother or your sweetheart, asks you, "What are you blue about anyway?" You cannot answer her because you do not yourself know. You have most of the things you want or are convinced that you are going to get them in the future, and you take pride and pleasure in your work, your friends, and your possessions. Yet over and over there comes to you the thought that perhaps after all life is hardly worth living.

You have once or twice talked it over with an intimate friend, but he had nothing to offer which you had not already thought of yourself. Probably when you are in such a mood you will get the greatest comfort from the great poets and novelists who have also felt the deep sadness of life and have been able to express it in words instead of in what your friends are accustomed to dub your "grouches."

Fortunately these periods of depression are a minor part of your life. Indeed many of your acquaintances think of you as one of the most genial and light-hearted men they know. You have many friends both among men and among women to whom you are loyal and generous, and you hold your friendships a long time. People in trouble come to you for advice and find you sympathetic. You are an energetic and vigorous worker and do well whether you are working for another person or as your own boss.

Key Number 125

SOME women are always looking for trouble, and you will probably find a wife some day who will not only take the risk of marrying you but will keep right on adoring you in spite of your sins. Let us hope her influence makes you better tempered.

As a matter of fact, if she is the right kind you will have a far happier time than you think you will. Of course people will wonder "how she stands him," and all the girls you did not marry will say how glad of it they are, but after a while the tune will change to "she's done wonders for him" and "he's really not as bad as he used to be" and so on.

One satisfaction you will have in life. People won't overlook you. You are the kind of he-man that attracts men, and whom women, alas, fall madly in love with. You will always be spoiled through life.

Two things, moreover, must be said for you. While you have your ups and downs of temperament, you do not go in for petty criticism; you may swear, but you don't carp. The other thing is that you are no weakling.

A third point for your comfort may be added. You will probably improve as you get older, especially if you see more of women. Seek out the kind that disapproves of you, as well as those romantic young things that are always flocking around you. Get to know strong-minded business women—preferably radicals—who are more interested in themselves than in you. It is not exactly necessary for you to marry that kind; but associate with them, and it will do you a lot of good.

Key Number 134

YOUR friends would be surprised if they knew what goes on in your mind. You live in two worlds, and the second world is marvelous because you made it yourself and in it you are king. Not literally king, because your imagination runs to other lines; perhaps adventurer in far-away lands or beach-comber on a South Sea island or master of industry. You people your second world with your friends, who are many, and wherever you go you carry your Dream Woman with you. No one knows about the Dream Woman, and wild horses could not drag her name out of you. In fact her name changes from time to time, and indeed she is usually a rather vague personality whom you would have a hard time to sketch, but always she is beautiful and kind and ardent and madly in love with you.

Has it ever occurred to you that the reason you do not push ahead faster in your career is because so much of your attention is turned to these beautiful unrealities? They rest you when you are tired; they cheer you when you are downhearted; but they don't buy shoes for the baby, and never will. You are ambitious, but you are not going ahead fast enough to suit you. You will go faster if you can turn your vivid imagination to actualities. Make your dreams work for you. Imagination lies back of all achievement. It creates poems, steam-engines, paintings, weaving-machines, great businesses, new ways of bookkeeping, time-saving devices, statues, and empires. Are you not somewhat extravagant to use so much of yours on dreams that can never come true?

Key Number 135

YOU are anxious to be a success and do not hesitate to plunge into a new business, but after you have plunged you begin to question your judgment. Instead of going along on an even keel, you tend to roll somewhat unsteadily. It may be, however, that you will make your big hit some day, when you have given up expecting luck to lift you over the crest of each wave.

Do not hesitate to ask advice from your wife, if you have one. One who does not understand the intimacies of a business can often grasp its needs more readily than an expert who is hampered by his appreciation of minor difficulties.

You are always busy over something and find little time to loaf, but you prefer to do things in your own way. You are more interested in finding a new way to do something than you are in accomplishing a piece of work.

Do not hesitate to face everything squarely, especially the income tax.

Key Number 145

You have, or used to have before you were married, the reputation of falling in love with every girl you met and falling out of love with equal facility. Nobody knew about the Fairy Princess whom you have been seeking all your life and have never found. Sometimes you discovered one trait of her in a new acquaintance. This new girl had eyes of the right color, or the right inflection to her voice, or your way of thinking about things. But sooner or later you discovered that she possessed also qualities that no Fairy Princess ever showed. Each time it was a bitter disappointment to you. You never got used to the awakening. You grew cynical and decided that there are no Fairy Princesses among women.

Have you ever stopped to consider that women have the same experience when they look for a Prince Charming among men? We might as well accept the fact that Fairy Princesses and Prince Charmings are never found in the real world. Men and women who would rather be comfortable than broken-hearted make the best of this sad situation and learn to love the boresome, trying, disappointing creatures that human beings really are. If you can join this group of realists, you will find yourself happier in your work and in your human relationships. For you are not always as happy as the people around you believe you to be, since you have a marvelous ability to make others gay when you are most downhearted.

Key Number 234

ONCE they have overcome your slight inertia and persuaded you to go on the picnic, you are the life of the party and the one who makes it a success. You nearly always have a good time, so why do you tend to think at first that you won't go?

Another question: why didn't you make that chicken-coop you planned? Of course it may not have literally been a chicken-coop. Perhaps it was a radio set, but the point is that you wanted to make it and had all the necessary knowledge and then didn't.

The same thing may happen to you in business, so look out for it. You want money, and you ought to seize the opportunity to make it. Otherwise when you see other men moving into big houses and buying big cars you will be dissatisfied.

You are the kind who would use money wisely, for you are generous without being a spendthrift, and you are sensible about your own personal expenditures. You are not particularly interested in "wine, women, and song" as a general principle. (Which does not mean that you don't like women; on the contrary it means that you do—in the most appreciative way.)

You are really rather a dear. The people who brought you up did a good job.

CHARACTER STUDIES FOR MEN

Key Number 235

YOU would be utterly charming and completely satisfactory to yourself as well as others if only you —no, let us leave your only serious defect till the last; so many fine qualities crowd to the front. You always, as the old saying has it, carry a cheerful face. If one were reading your personality in proverbs, one would say you put the right foot out of bed first when you get up. You put that same best foot forward during the day. And, in a final quaint phrase, when you swing your foot, the ball goes. In brief, you are firm on your feet, and marching onward to victory.

You will reach the place you have started for, and you have yourself a pretty clear notion of where that goal is located, although you do not say much about it. You may knock down a few persons who try to stop you, but you are not by nature a cruel person.

But—here is the lack in your character—unless you change your attitude toward women you will not be happy in marriage; no, not though you marry five times. Or seven. You have a profound distrust of women, although they attract you. You can't keep away from them, but you can't get along with them either. Many men are like that. They unconsciously select untrustworthy women and deduce that all are like them, or else they are unconsciously so hostile to women that they stir up hostility in return. You have a good brain, and if you turn intelligence toward this trait, you can correct it. If you do not change your attitude, Heaven help the woman who marries you!

Key Number 245

YOU have so many extraordinarily fine characteristics that you can surely alter the one flaw that is obvious in your personality. Let us talk first about your excellences. You are probably working for some one else. Your answers do not indicate that you have your own business, although this is not quite clear. You have the attributes which qualify a man to climb from one position to another higher and higher until he achieves at last an executive office in which he is responsible to the board of directors alone. You fortunately lack that uneasy quality which makes it necessary for a man to strike out for himself regardless of whether he can succeed or not, because he is unable to coöperate or to accept supervision.

Coöperation is highly developed in you, and you have never hated supervision because you do your work so well. If you are now well along in your career, you will know in your heart that this praise is justified, even though you have not done all that you intended to do. If you are just starting, go on with courage, confident that you will pass many who began the race at the same time with you.

In your business or professional life, you meet chiefly men. This is fortunate, for you have not learned to get along with women satisfactorily. The flaw in your personality is simply a little stupidity in your intelligence. You expect more of women than you do of men, and you are resentful when they fall short of your impossible ideal. If you expect less, you will find that they are not such a bad sort after all.

Key Number 345

YOUR dreams grow as fast as Jack's bean-stalk, forming a strong ladder to which you could mount to reach your goal. Why don't you climb when you are so well fitted to succeed? Instead of getting to the place where you would like to go, you sit at the foot of the bean-stalk which you have planted and dream and wish and lose yourself in fancies.

Perhaps you have never fully realized how much ability you have. You may be the type that takes life easily and needs to be prodded into action. Men like that are apt to marry energetic women who will make them do what they know they ought to do. It is somewhat curious that men who unconsciously choose wives strong in the qualities which they themselves lack are resentful even when they are availing themselves of their wives' strength. They would be much happier if they could admit to themselves that they need and demand the goadings which anger them.

You have the excellent quality of keeping your annoyance to yourself and preserving a cheerful manner when things go against you. You frequently find it difficult to laugh when your heart is heavy. It would be a far lighter heart if you could work more steadily toward your ambitions instead of wishing they would come true of themselves.

Key Number 1234

ARE you always planning to break away next month? And are you restrained by the feeling that the people who hold you back really know better than you?

If you are still quite young you are probably undecided whether to choose a practical or artistic career, but the artistic will doubtless win, even though you enjoy mechanical things. You will probably develop more between the ages of thirty and forty than between twenty and thirty, the period when most men make their greatest strides.

You have a lovable personality, in spite of being irritable, and a generous spirit toward others. You are extremely sensitive but not touchy. Of course you are always in love.

Your dependence on the people around you comes from your hatred of routine duties. You want others to remind you of them, but you are annoyed when they do.

You might pose a trifle, but fundamentally you are genuine, with real appreciation of subtleties in art, strong ambition, and plenty of character. In literature you like humor, tenderness, and sincerity. You have a most generous admiration for other artists, and a wholesome attitude toward women.

Key Number 1235

WHAT you say goes. What you start you finish. You have little patience with irresolute and lazy persons because you yourself are so self-reliant and energetic. You are the type of man who carries through great enterprises which bring riches to him and more comfort to millions of others. Men of your sort, when they reach the goal toward which they have climbed through long and toilsome years, are often surprised to find how little it means to them after all. The reason for this is that in the stress and strain of the struggle they have not taken time to be considerate and generous toward others. Their minds have been on outwitting their rivals and getting all the work possible out of their employees. Some of them have not even put their attention on making friends of their wives, assuming quite wrongly that once a wife, always a friend.

These are the men who have trouble with their workmen, encounter strikes at crucial points, become involved in lawsuits, and are served with divorce papers. Take thought while there is yet time and cultivate the softer side of your nature. Begin now to greet your acquaintances cordially, to interest yourself sincerely in the lives of your friends, to look upon women as friendly creatures, to speak words of admiration instead of criticism, and to give generous praise where it is due. Do not forget that recreation in its place is as important as industry and ambition.

Key Number 1245

WHAT a lot of energy you waste! Some of it goes into disliking people; some of it goes into planning schemes that you have not the slightest intention of carrying out; and some of it goes into carrying out impulses that are futile. You really do not care about the things you do or do the things you care about.

And yet, in spite of all this, you have great strength of character. You are hard to influence—for good or evil. Stubborn? If you ever had an argument with a mule, you'd win.

So just face yourself and admit that something ought to be done about it. Admit that that girl who recently told you a few plain truths about yourself was right! You have so much strength that you can afford to be gentle. To yield now and then would not make you weaker in the eyes of the world, but stronger, more lovable.

Of course you might feel that your impregnable citadel had been taken if you ever let any one gain your confidence, but provided it were the right person you would be happier afterward. For you want to be liked—more than you will admit to yourself. But let your friendships have something more than an emotional basis; for that way, for you, lies disillusionment.

Key Number 1345

THE people who call you vacillating and fickle do not know what they are talking about. You only seem so to those who do not understand you. You might as well accept the fact that the majority never will realize the sort of a person you are, for you have an unusual combination of qualities. Perhaps one woman loves you enough to bear with your many trying traits for the sake of something fine which she vaguely feels is there; maybe that woman is waiting for you somewhere in the future. But you have a most unfortunate tendency to show the worst side of your personality at times when it does you the most harm. This is a part of a contrariness of your nature, and it makes it very hard for any woman to bear with you. You blame the unfortunate outcome on the woman, and sometimes it may be her fault; but usually it is because you draw too heavily on the patience, affection, and comprehension of any one with whom you are closely associated.

All this hurts you deeply, and you sometimes resolve to go away and live utterly alone, where you will not be so constantly disappointed in people. Is one of your favorite day-dreams of a desert island with all the comforts of home but no relatives?

You know your own faults better than any one else, although you have not realized how unhappy they have made you. Choose the opposite of the trait that makes you the most trouble and develop this new characteristic. If you like the result, try the same recipe on other phases of your personality.

Key Number 2345

YOURS is a rather curious character combining some almost contradictory traits. You have the business man's temperament and the poet's heart, for one thing. Part of the time you seem like a typical hustler who will make the Rotary Club early; then you suddenly begin to wonder if you would not rather give it all up and go off to the South Seas, or some equally distant spot. You know few women really well; perhaps none at all. You have any number of acquaintances but tend to keep on the surface with them, and it hardly occurs to you that women have their problems just as you have. It is just possible that you have two conceptions of women: the imaginary woman, to whom you could open your heart; and the real woman, to whom you have given very little attention. You think you understand her of course, but that is only because you assume that there is nothing intricate about her.

With men you are more communicative and very popular, especially in your buoyant moods. You are apt to overwork, though, and when you are tired you get discouraged.

Beware the influence of moonlight! Let both your selves sit in conference before undertaking anything important. In other words, be sure that what you do appeals as reasonable to the practical side of you, and also let it satisfy that part of you that wants more out of life than worldly success.

Key Number 12345

YOU have the qualities that make for spectacular success, but you are not happy. Probably your dejection does not show, for you are not the kind to wail your sorrows to the crowd. You share your gaiety and keep your depression to yourself.

You are likely to be one of the most important men of your community by the time you are forty, for you can see what should be done, make plans for accomplishing it, and direct other men. You are better as a promoter than as a day-by-day executive. You are always thinking up new plans, and sometimes you want to upset affairs that are going very well in order to experiment with making them go better. You get sat on by your superiors when you make such suggestions. You lose heart then and swear to yourself that you never again will attempt to beat sense into their brains, and you fall into a black mood and hate the world.

You are drawn to women, but because you distrust them you are always at odds with them, and that adds to your unhappiness. If you could only accept bosses and women as a part of the scheme of life, and adjust yourself to their deficiencies, since you cannot change them, you would save yourself many a heartache. Some of the schemes which you have put through with enormous effort would have gone easily if you had studied more carefully the personalities with which you had to deal.

QUESTIONS FOR WOMEN

For directions see page 1

GROUP 1

A—Would you like to go up in an airplane?

B—If you heard a noise at night would you get up to investigate it?

C—Are you among "the first by whom the new is tried"?

D—Would you paint your house bright blue if you felt like it?

E—Would you interfere with a woman who was slapping her baby on the street?

GROUP 2

A—Do you get hysterical?

B—Would you walk five blocks to see a parade?

C—Do you cry at the theater?

D—Do many people "get on your nerves"?

E—Do you have strong likes and dislikes?

GROUP 3

A—Do you avoid asking advice if possible?

B—Do you object to giving in for the sake of peace?

C—Are your mistakes your own fault?

D—Do you read what you like rather than what you are told you should?

E—Does achievement gratify you more than admiration?

GROUP 4

A—Do you prefer to make a decision rather than "wait to see what breaks"?

B—Are you as successful as your friends?

C—Do you trust your own judgment?

D—Can you forget your social "breaks"?

E—Do you answer these questions easily rather than tend to quibble?

GROUP 5

A—If a woman you dislike is wearing a becoming hat, are you willing to tell her so?

B—Do you like three of the last five people you talked with? (Present company excepted.)

C—Do you like most of your friends' friends?

D—Do you think the world is growing better?

E—Do you tell white lies to make people happy?

KEY NUMBERS FOR WOMEN

CHARACTER STUDIES FOR WOMEN

Key Number 0

THERE is no blinking the fact that you are an old-fashioned clinging vine, and it is very lucky for you that a large proportion of men still prefer that sort. If you have married a man who wants a sturdy oak of a wife, you are out of luck, my dear; and the best you can do is to endure the situation in the quiet, placid manner which is your greatest charm.

If you are not yet married, look for a man who will be a kind protector and a good provider. If you do not marry, get yourself into a steady job where faithfulness and industry count for more than aggressiveness, for there is not in you one half-ounce of that disquieting quality called ambition.

Now, here is a gentle warning. A woman who relies on others as much as you do must find a way of repaying the debt she owes. No, keeping the house and spanking the children is not enough. She must pay in gratitude and love. She must learn to say aloud all the kind thoughts that come into her mind while she keeps critical remarks from coming out. A clinging vine may be poison ivy, or it may be honeysuckle, yielding up fragrance to the whole garden.

Key Number 1

YOU are most fortunate in your philosophical temperament and your calmness in what would be to others an occasion for hysteria. High-strung men are particularly attracted to you on this account. But it is possible that you are too limited in your friendships. If you were less sensitive to people's bad qualities you could more enjoy their excellences.

Your greatest handicap is lack of belief in yourself. You overestimate the ability of others, thus underestimating yourself. Those on whom you can lean may have less actual stability than you have. Try standing on your own feet. Get an impersonal view of your characteristics and let the admirable ones be an incentive to improving the poorer ones. Your finest quality is your courage. This is the engine that will pull you over sandy roads of monotony, through swamps of despair, up hills of difficulty, until you finally reach a height from which you behold a glorious future.

Key Number 2

YOU are something of a dreamer, seeing yourself in the glamorous atmosphere of fame or luxury, the center of all eyes, the adored one of a countless throng of admirers. Next time you find yourself slipping into that dream, why not ask yourself how you are going to bring it about? Are you planning to marry the Prince of Wales? That would certainly give you the prominence you would like to enjoy, but as a practical solution of your problems it has its limitations. Suppose you try something easier; not marriage necessarily, for perhaps you would be just as happy unmarried, but something that would bring beauty into your life. For you are a beauty lover.

As a matter of fact, in spite of your dreams you are not really ambitious; you would like to be famous, or else a woman of wealth, living in luxury in vast palatial rooms, but not if it involves doing something about it. Perhaps, after all, you enjoy your dreams as much as you would their fulfilment. The ambitious ones seldom have dreams that they cannot conceivably realize; the dreamers seldom confine themselves to dreams that they can make come true. Only a woman who is very charming is likely to develop a personality of the kind you seem to have.

Key Number 3

A FAVORITE grievance that we hear expressed every time a new invention comes into the home is: "I was born fifty years too soon." But you were born fifty years too late! Can you not see yourself as a pioneer woman going stanchly on to face the things you fear? Perhaps it is this grim realization that life must be grappled with, hardship endured, and fears overcome that makes you a little out of sympathy with the flippancies and frivolities of the present generation. Dancing girls seem to you like butterflies on the edge of a volcano; to you gilded youth in motor-cars seems to be steering headlong for a precipice.

Have you sometimes wished that you were a man, with the thought that then your gift for organization would be given free play? If this is the case, you are using your sex as an excuse for failure. As a matter of fact you have fewer handicaps to overcome on the road to success than most of us, for you get your way rather easily. You do not have to go into hysterics over it either; in fact hysterics are not in your line, and you have no interest in staging a scene in which you would play the chief rôle.

It is probable, in fact, that you have already achieved a good deal. You have learned to stand on your own feet and to be independent; in short, you have learned to grow up when you would have preferred to remain a protected child. The rôle of the pioneer woman suits you chiefly because you would like to have been the protected wife of the pioneer man. You would have admired his courage, resourcefulness, strength, and manliness; and you would have liked to direct him, just as you would like to drive an engine. You would rather spur others on to courageous deeds than do them yourself. But remember that if you want your husband to be a pioneer man it is a rather selfish desire on your part. It might be very much better for you if he were quite the opposite. But not for him!

Key Number 4

YOU begin every piece of work superbly. The master mind and the craftsman's hand are both yours. Your comrades admire you frantically—for a little while. You slump in the very middle of your achievement because you are bored and something new attracts your attention. Again your start is magnificent; again you don't hold out. The plodding tortoise seldom finds you at the goal you could so easily have reached. You do not realize that it is this characteristic which has caused you so much trouble. You blame other people for your failures. You have all the qualities that make for success except staying-power.

When your type goes in for marriage, the number of husbands is greater than the number of golden weddings.

The lack of completion in any phase of your life is what makes you so restless. Sometimes a woman like you is eaten up by jealousy of much inferior women who have got ahead by sticking to one line. Only by turning your energy toward one aim and holding to that will you find your rightful satisfaction in life.

Key Number 5

A GREAT many people expect special concessions from the world because they suffer from shyness, sensitiveness, and a retiring disposition. They want to be taken care of like children after they have grown up. They do not trust their own judgment.

The whole success or failure of your future life depends on your getting rid of the feeling that you are not as good as your neighbor. Because you are exceptionally just by nature, you have leaned over backward in giving others their due. Your own sincerity has made you blind to the fact that the showiness of many people who impress you as successful is a large bluff. You should learn to ignore everything about yourself that is unfavorable and concentrate on your good qualities, which far outnumber your weaknesses. Think of all the kindly things you have done during the past year. Think of the faithful way in which you have kept all your promises, whether other people were doing their share or not.

Think of your good points continually so that you

completely forget the diffidence that is holding you back. (The fact that you frequently tell yourself that you are superior to your neighbors in certain respects —perhaps mentally or socially—is only another manifestation of your sense of inferiority. Do not dwell so much on your superiority, but forget your inferiority.) Incidentally, your appearance is probably far more attractive than you think it is.

Decide what you wish to do, make practical plans for doing it, and then take the first steps regardless of whether you expect to succeed or not. Walk straight up to the job even if it is failure that awaits you. If you always have to carry doubt and worry on your back, you will find the burden a severe handicap, and it will not excuse you from bearing your part in the world's work.

Key Number 12

ALTHOUGH you at first appear easy to get along with, you do not care for the average person. You prefer a few close friends to many acquaintances. This of course has its advantages, but are you not making the mistake of sheltering yourself from the world too much? Do not your prejudices keep you from seeing that every one has something to give you and something to receive from you, in spite of a few unlovely traits that force themselves on your attention? You would be less lonely if you tempered your critical judgments with compassion.

Strangely enough one of your best qualities is usually considered a failing—your unstable and excitable temperament. While as a rule emotionalism is no virtue, yet this trait shows that you are alive and alert. Temper your high spirit with kindliness, and you will find that instead of making lines in your face, it will come out as vivacity instead of irritation. Seek out all humanizing influences—dogs or cats, if you like them, flowers, the theater, music, or out-of-door life. By all means buy a new frock if you feel like it. Try to make yourself happy, not spasmodically happy, but daily and hourly more serene. If you will face the facts—as you probably will, for you are almost a Spartan in courage—you will probably admit that it is only when you are happy yourself that you really want to see others happy.

Key Number 13

WOMEN like you are sometimes more unhappy because of their good qualities than on account of their faults, for your excellences are those which society admires in a man and resents in a woman. You are like Napoleon leading his troops into battle, like a great doctor fighting a pestilence, but you are a complete failure as a flapper or a member of a church sewing-circle. Two courses lie open to you: either accept your destiny of being different from the popular model of woman, or make peace with the world by developing conscientiously the feminine side of your nature—courtesy, interest in others, kindness, and like qualities that belong both to a gentlewoman and to a perfect gentle knight.

The latter course—that of being as much like women as you conveniently can—has the advantage because every one hates to be obviously different. The resentment which comes between you and other individuals is anger at their attitude toward your outspoken aggressiveness. If you can cultivate the so-called womanly traits, women and more especially men will cease to fear you and will admire your forthrightness.

Key Number 14

YOU are willing to bear your share of the burdens of life; and you do not ask in return, as so many do, for a blare of trumpets to precede you. Your fortitude helps you to carry on when you would much rather rest. But while you do not want to lead, neither do you especially like to see others lead. You are not the first to applaud the general as he rides by in glory; indeed you are rather grudging when it comes to giving others their due. It would not hurt you to praise people a little more. You will find that it makes you feel more warmly toward them and it makes them feel more warmly toward you.

You desire independence, but you do not fight for it. You trust your own judgment but do not follow it. You have the courage of your convictions but are too indifferent to do anything about it.

Men do not mean as much to you as they do to the average woman; yet in spite of your cold-heartedness you are rather attractive to men, especially in business relations. They know that they can depend upon you.

I'VE GOT YOUR NUMBER

You would do well to make more friends and really try to keep them. You are in danger of becoming too introspective and too indifferent to other people. Remember, those who are popular have to work for their popularity, not once, but every day of their lives.

Key Number 15

CAN you make a decision? Or do you allow others to decide for you? It looks as if that were your weakest point—a tendency to lean on others' judgment, a willingness to let others guide your life. A girl of this type is in danger of remaining under her parents' control too long, allowing them to choose her husband for her or even to discourage a perfectly good suitor because they want to keep her at home.

A woman with your traits makes the best possible sort of a wife for a strong-willed, adventurous, affectionate man. You would follow your husband without hesitation to icebergs or deserts or jungles and count the comforts of civilization well lost if only you could be with him.

You do not make much show of your affections, deep as they are. You are perhaps a little too placid, although that quality is a restful one on which highstrung natures enjoy leaning. You are a tigress protecting her cubs when your loved ones are menaced, and since your love is broad and generous there are many who call you blessed.

Key Number 23

WHAT are you afraid of anyway? Mice and men and thunder-storms, or poverty and sickness and unknown misfortunes? Snap your finger at the first group and be philosophical about the others, for worry summons troubles about you as a dinner-bell calls summer boarders to a meal. I will say this for you: you tackle life vigorously, but Old Man Worry sits on your shoulders and chuckles because he makes the struggle so hard for you. The problems of work and love and bringing up children and getting comfortable shoes that aren't too ugly are difficult enough without having half one's energy diverted into chronic anxiety.

Do you know that sometimes a woman is able to make a dark emotion over into a feeling as glorious as the sun at midday? There was once a woman who only partly liked her husband. The part she did not like grew bigger and bigger, and the part she did like became a dwarf. Something had to be done, and this is what she did. She made out a list of her husband's good qualities and of every advantage she gained by being married to him. She read that list over and over as if it were the prayer-book every time she felt hateful toward him. By the time the paper wore out something very curious had happened: she had fallen in love with her husband! She discovered that the man with whom she had been living for fifteen years was an entirely different person from what she had supposed, and that she adored him.

Key Number 24

ONCE in a while you feel that you ought to make a speech. Perhaps you have a chance to make it to the public; if so, you are fortunate, and so is your family. Of course you are frightened to death at making speeches, but you do it because you feel that you can make a speech as well as anybody; and so why shouldn't you? You feel that you are right in what you have to say, and so why shouldn't people listen to you?

They should, but before you make your speeches (whether formal or informal) be sure to marshal all your facts. Find out beforehand just what the other person's point of view is, so that when he presents it you will have your answer ready. Put yourself in his place, and see all the reason that you can in his arguments, so that your answer will convince rather than annoy him.

You are usually ready to take up arms for your friends, which is an endearing quality, but be sure that partizanship does not overbalance your judgment. If you could spread your feeling thin so that it would cover more people and be less intense, it might be better for you.

Your energy and quick championship of the oppressed make you a person who will be appreciated in an hour of need. By the way, you may be glad to hear that you are the type of woman who gets an unusually nice husband.

Key Number 25

DID you ever know a woman who was so fond of her children that she could not let them have a good time? That may be your danger. And then, when they break away, as they must, how lost you will feel! Please try not to hold so tightly to your loved ones, because you do it not only to save them from danger, but also to save yourself from feeling lost. Remember it is only children who get panicky when they find themselves alone. You should train yourself to look your fears in the eye, and they will slink away.

The root of your trouble is that you do not appreciate yourself. You would rather be guided than lead. And yet you have such splendid qualities, such unselfish impulses and ready sympathy, and such unexpected energy in helping those who are in trouble. It gives you great satisfaction, does it not, to feel that some life has been made happier through your efforts? Probably, for one thing, you are something of a match-maker, and like nothing better than to watch your deep-laid schemes blossom.

I'VE GOT YOUR NUMBER

Your chief charm is a childlike trusting spirit which makes people want to protect you. And you dress to suit the part. You have an April temperament, balmy one minute and stormy the next. If you will learn by experience that most of your fears are unfounded, and face the world a little more courageously, you will find that it is more satisfactory to live your own life than to be an accessory—however valuable—of some other life. Good luck to you!

Key Number 34

WHERE other people are afraid, you go ahead confidently, although you get panicky over simple matters not worth noticing. You really cannot be classified either as a brave woman or as a coward, because you jump from one side to the other so fast. If you could only mix the two traits you would be just right.

Your poise and your way of going ahead in the direction you choose are fine; but are you not a little inclined to elbow others out of the way? It may be true that they are blocking progress, but be a little more patient with them, for they can't help being blockheads.

You are a curious mixture of traits all jumbled up together. Some of your finest characteristics have been pushed into the background by your passion for getting ahead—shall one say for having your own way? Bring forward your generosity, comprehension of others, altruism, and high ideals, and be the woman that only you can be.

Key Number 35

NOBODY guesses how hard it sometimes is for you to keep on "doing the next thing." Often it seems to you as if life rose up against you like a tidal wave. You shut your eyes and hold your breath, and after eons of smothering desolation you find yourself on the crest, not broken but triumphant. Were you a hysterical woman you would long ago have gone under.

It is strange that you have never learned the lesson of self-confidence from your many victories. Count up your successes and forget your failures. You present a valiant front, and no one sees that you are really trembling. The tragedy is that there is no need for your uneasiness. You will always surmount the wave.

Love of your family and of your wide circle of friends is the motive that inspires most of your actions. You express this devotion more in deeds than in words, and this has given you something of a reputation for being cold. If you can bring yourself to be more demonstrative, people will immediately begin to be drawn to you and sing loudly praises of the real You.

Key Number 45

MOST people like you, although you are not faultless! You lack the inspiring rushes of enthusiasm that would carry you over difficulties, but on the other hand you never throw fits when you are displeased. Indeed you are not easily annoyed; you take life calmly on the whole. One hopes you are married, for you are the type who loves her children but does not let them put anything over on her. You have enough timidity to give a husband the sense of protecting you, but you will never be a burden.

You are efficient and adaptable, not self-willed; ready to let others make the decisions, and able to adjust yourself to their wishes. You know your good qualities, and this gives you confidence. If you work for a living you will probably reach a moderately high position, for you are not afraid to tackle new tasks; but not the highest, for you lack aggressiveness. The other workers in the office will like you and have a tendency to let you help them too much. Be on your guard against allowing yourself to be drawn into other people's affairs. If you made your decisions more firmly and showed more energy in bringing the good things of life your way, you would be very nearly an ideal woman.

Key Number 123

Do you eat the candied cherry on the top of the cake first or save it till the last? At the end of this discourse you will find a plump red cherry, but first comes a fault that you should correct. You have not allowed your sympathies and your affections to flow in a broad deep stream toward the people who make up your neighborhood, your city, your nation, your world. You have vigorous emotions. You could be a great lover. Instead it sometimes seems as if you were in training to be a great hater! Your lack of outgoing love may be due to a feeling that you have not a fair share of comfort, good times, talents, social position, and happiness. You may be bitter toward those who have more.

You possess two fine traits that should bring you satisfaction: you are strong and courageous. That is the cherry I promised you—two cherries—strength and courage. A woman who has those characteristics is able to cope with any situation. She can make herself all over. You can, if you choose, become the finest of human beings—a woman whose love goes round the world and reaches to the stars above.

Key Number 124

YOU are not one to yearn for things that you can buy around the corner. If you want anything, you usually go and get it—at least you *decide* to go and get it. Your weakness is not indecision, but the lack of initiative to carry out your decisions.

Do you tend to look down on the mass of humanity? Do you wish the world were made up of "fewer and better people"? Have you ever so far fallen from grace as to think of a crowd of people as "cattle"? If you have, it is clear that the thing which keeps you from realizing the best that is in you is indifference. You have not sufficiently used your imagination on other people, each one of whom can be a sympathetic character if you can look at him from the proper angle.

You have splendid qualities otherwise: readiness to face an issue, plenty of warmth (but focused on a few persons) and—oh, rare virtue!—the ability to look at others through level eyes that are not lifted in admiration. If you fall into the opposite fault of looking down on those whom you consider beneath you, it is a fault easier to overcome.

Key Number 125

HAVE you ever wondered why it is that you do things for others which you would never think of doing for yourself? You would beg, borrow, almost steal for a loved one, while you can hardly bring yourself to accept the necessities of life from another's hand.

The reason is simple. You have not a very high opinion of yourself, in spite of all the pleasant words people say of you, and you have a guilty feeling that you haven't any right to the good things of life. So you enjoy them through getting them for your friends and family or any one who needs help. You are applying a cure to an emotional sickness from which you suffer—the sickness of self-depreciation, of lack of confidence, poise, and self-reliance. You gain a justifiable pride and sense of power in "helping lame dogs over the stile." Keep doing this, but to your philanthropy add a little attention to yourself. If you are married, get your husband to unite with you in budgeting the income, so that a definite amount will be spent on your clothes. If you are a wage-earner, set yourself to win a higher salary or a better position. If you are unmarried, see how many men you can make propose to you in the next year, but don't marry more than one of them.

Key Number 134

NOW you are about to be told, straight off the bat, what you have to guard against. Don't be annoyed, please. If you are not very careful indeed, you are going to steam-roller your friends, family, and the other committee members.

You do things so easily and efficiently that people instinctively turn to you for advice and help. In your eagerness to aid, you are likely to try to make them do what is good for them instead of encouraging them to do what they want to do.

If you were a man you would be a master of industry or a political boss, and everything would be all right. But you are a woman, and it will avail you little to make your home as lovely as a bower of roses, as neat as a pin, and as regular as clockwork, if you boss your family. For people will be hostile, and that cuts you. And, oh, be very, very careful about your husband who is or is to be! He may resent your positive character even while he admires it. Look for his strong points, and let him lead half the time. You may have then the most wonderful form of love—the love of married comrades.

Key Number 135

YOU are one of those who desire to protect humanity, but whose sphere of influence is limited by your own inability to express the loving-kindness that is one of your fundamental traits. Wise, strong, and generous, you lack only the initiative and self-confidence to undertake the things you plan.

Do not let the pleasure of looking down on yourself impair the dignity of your soul; do not refuse to admit your own intrinsic merits. For you are the kind whose influence is needed. Though you may seem to others a trifle cold and forbidding, you have a compassionate heart and a stanch spirit. Free from emotionalism, you can look fairly at any question that does not involve an estimate of your own personality. Your good-will and kindliness will carry you farther than the spasmodic warmth that you probably admire so much in others.

You are inclined to be shy, but you have the courage of your convictions when your sense of justice is outraged, and you can come to the front with the best of them.

I'VE GOT YOUR NUMBER

Some people believe in the theory that each person is at his or her best at a certain age and in one or another of the human relationships. If this is true, you would probably be at your best between the ages of thirty and forty. Your best qualities are the kind that would be most apparent in middle life, and your most successful rôle will be that of mother. This is indeed a rare trait.

Key Number 145

A PICTURE of you might be called "Lady with a Clear Conscience." It would show you with a gentle mouth somewhat contradicted by resolute eyes. It would show you with a calm brow and a feminine chin. It would show you as the kind of woman who is called "easy-going," except when a moral issue is involved. Then, roused from your natural calm, you take matters into your own hand and call up the S.P.C.A. or do whatever else is necessary.

You would be at your best as a married woman, but you are not necessarily the kind that marries early. Your traits do not appeal so much to young men as to older ones. Children like you, and you would make an excellent teacher. If you have any children you will find them easy to manage if they are like you rather than like their father, for the kind of man you pick out will have a will of his own. It is just as well that you have plenty of self-control.

You are not afraid to carry out your own ideas because you are sure that they are right, but you would prefer to have some one else do the actual work. When people are in trouble, however, you are among the first to offer consolation and practical suggestions. You doubtless had a pleasant home during your childhood and were proud of your parents. You admire your husband too, if you have one; indeed your domestic relations have always been harmonious. Perhaps this is because your character shows the somewhat rare combination of self-confidence, a generous spirit, and a disposition to see the other person's point of view.

Key Number 234

DID it ever occur to you that as a free and independent adult you can do pretty much as you like? Instead of fighting others, why do you not go ahead and do what you want to do? As a matter of fact there are two reasons why you don't: first, because the plans you want to carry out are plans for other people as well as for yourself, and they have their own ideas about what is best for them; and, second, because you are afraid to follow your own advice. You feel sure that your ideas are good, yet you can be dissuaded from carrying them out, and then, when it is proved that you were right after all, you want to blame those who held you back.

You have a vivid personality and make yourself felt. You are dominant and self-confident; both are excellent qualities if accompanied by good judgment and a friendly feeling toward others. If you are a little inclined to look at yourself as the center of the universe, it is only because you are very much interested in yourself, and that is commendable. But try once in a while to think of other persons as the heroes and heroines of their own stories, and it may help you to gain a more tender human spirit.

Even though you have abundant energy, you waste too much of it in fighting individuals both in your home and out of it. Windmills may look like enemies, but they are really quite harmless.

Key Number 235

YOU sound as if you were a trifle timid, though I cannot see why a woman of your personality should ever doubt herself. Of course you make mistakes, but most mistakes are not really very serious, and a large number of them can be corrected. Why do you distrust your ability to deal with life?

People are fond of you. Confess they are, although they may sometimes tell you that your heart runs away with your head, and that you are looking for trouble, and they may give you sage advice that worries you because you have no intention of following it.

Finest of all your traits is the way your interest goes out to others, so that what happens to them is almost as if it happened to you. The pleasures that come to you you cannot enjoy unless you share them.

On second thoughts, I believe that even that fine characteristic is not so admirable as the way you go ahead along what you think is the right course in spite of doubts and worries. I take back what I said about your timidity, for you advance when you are afraid, and that is the greatest courage of all.

Key Number 245

YOU have been exceptionally fortunate in your early training. Traits that might have handicapped you are for the most part buried, and you face the world with assurance.

Very affectionate, friendly toward the neighbors, and demonstrative toward those at home, you are the kind of woman who is usually considered an "ideal wife" because of the warm atmosphere which you create and the efficiency of your management.

Your greatest weakness is a certain timidity, physical rather than mental, due perhaps to a too comfortable environment and sheltered life. This does not, however, indicate in your case any tendency to retire to the background. Perhaps you have yourself noticed the contradictory characteristics that make you sometimes lead and at other times run away from situations that call for courageous handling.

Key Number 345

How nice you are to your friends! You love to invite them to tea and plan little surprises for them, and you are very likely to remember their birthdays. Usually you appear as the perfect hostess, calmly at ease, but you yourself know that your smile sometimes conceals a heartache. It is not so much things that have happened that disturb you, as the things that you fear may happen. You are always anxious about the health and safety of those who are dearest to you.

Your affections are strongly centered perhaps on one person, and you are willing to sacrifice others for the sake of the loved one.

You have aptitude for business but probably prefer a sheltered life. Your moral standards are high, and you are not afraid to stand up for what you believe is right. But are you not something of a pussycat when it comes to staying home by the fire? But, then, there is no reason to go out into the wind and rain unless you have an adventurous spirit—or an unhappy home. And yours is likely to be happy, for people like you who want to make other people happy are very likely to succeed.

Key Number 1234

NOTHING will surprise you more than to hear of your worst fault, for very likely you have always thought of the opposite trait as your greatest virtue. In spite of the fact that you are of a warm emotional temperament, in spite of the wideness of your circle of friends, you cannot be put down as "one who loves his fellow-men." In flashes you think of the man in the street as your friend, but for the most part he means less to you than a tree. You are, however, exceptionally fond of trees. Very likely there is something about trees among the poems you have written.

It is hard to give sufficient praise to your fine qualities, the decisiveness of character that will bring you success, your fearless attitude toward the world, and your appreciation of the worth-while things of life. You are generous, too, and like to do the treating. But your generosity is rather impulsive. You help the weak because they are weak, not because you love them. You do not yourself worry, nor understand people who do.

If you are married, or thinking of getting married, remember that your husband is a personality as well as a husband. For except for that rather alarming, and rather fascinating, savage streak and tendency to know everything, you are a really fine woman. You do not realize yourself how near you come to being ideal.

Key Number 1235

POOR thing! You think you have to "grin and bear it." Not that you are afraid to cut the ties that bind you, but you are too tender-hearted to risk hurting people's feelings. Also you want to be loved, and you think that the way to be loved is to be docile. Yours is a peculiarly strong and fine character, with all the qualities to make a happy successful woman, except that you feel obliged to accept what life gives you. You are too polite to Life. (Were you, perhaps, brought up with an undue emphasis on politeness?)

As you grow older, things are sure to improve for you, for as your character strengthens you will begin to see that there is no reason why you should endure hardship. If you have the strength for endurance, you have the strength for action, and in few cases is endurance necessary. Remember it is not courage you lack so much as self-confidence.

Your home life is very happy or very unhappy or both alternately; for your affections are strong, and yet you want to be free—a difficult combination.

Your business life, if you have one, ought to be more serene and very successful. You have the qualities that make women succeed in business, which, by the way, are feminine qualities. You are not envious, and your outlook is wholesome. You think rightly, or pleasantly, on most subjects. You are cheerful, popular, and optimistic, especially on the surface. You do not waste much time thinking about your enemies.

You are extremely popular with men, and also with women. And that means a great deal. For when both men and women agree on a person there is little chance for argument.

Key Number 1245

You have many warm friends and a few warm enemies, for yours is a type that people respond to strongly either one way or the other. At least you never need be afraid of being disregarded!

You have the courage of your convictions, and the only danger is that your convictions may not be sound. Perhaps you should ask advice more, even though you hate to do it. If you were not such a distinctly feminine type (with such a feminine method of getting your own way), you might be called dominating; as it is, people are usually indulgent toward you where they would be resentful toward other women who went ahead as you do. But they know that you have a warm heart, and they admire your courage.

Your danger, of course, is that some day you will upset the apple-cart by a sudden burst of temper. The thing you should guard against is nervousness, and the way to control that is to rest. You probably say that you cannot rest, but any one can say that. If you overwork, you have to rest in the end, somewhere or somehow, for you can't tax nature beyond her strength. Isn't it better to plan wisely when and where you will rest, instead of letting circumstances decide it for you?

Key Number 1345

NOTHING gets on your nerves. You can work under handicaps that would make the average woman rise in wrath and leave the house. If your gifts are mental, you are the type that might be very successful on a college faculty, where your ability and calm temperament would make you a real force. If, on the other hand, it is chiefly in your home that you shine, you are even more fortunate, for once your interest is centered on your home you can make it a home to be proud of. But do not try to be both a business woman and a home-maker. If you have a career before you, give some one else the housework to do— or it won't get done.

Perhaps your finest trait is loyalty. Your natural desire is to like people and to keep on liking them as long as you possibly can. You are distinctly disappointed when they fall short of what you thought they were.

If it were not for your loving heart there might be the danger that you would dominate your husband, but your common sense and natural generosity have doubtless steered you away from this danger. There are few people who can equal you in the traits that make up a fine, firm, and courageous character softened by the magic of kindliness.

Key Number 2345

PEOPLE go to you for sympathy, for yours is not only whole-souled but made practical by your faculty for discriminating criticism and sound advice. If you are still in your early twenties or younger you are probably popular with the boys, for you are not an unreasonable creature who has to be kept in a good temper. Although you have a chin of your own, you are willing to allow other people to have chins too; in fact in an emergency you are only too glad to have some one around who can help you through.

You like a good time so much that in order to get it you can overcome some of the little-girl fears that you have not quite outgrown. Try to do that, for timidity is one of your very few weaknesses.

Domesticity appeals to you, but so does a career. The only thing that would worry you in undertaking a new venture would be the thought that some power which you could not control might upset your plans. You do not distrust your own judgment or your own ability, but you are nervous about possible accidents.

I'VE GOT YOUR NUMBER

Be careful not to marry some one who wants to rediscover the North Pole. You never could settle down to your own work if your husband were far away.

Key Number 12345

ONE question you should ask yourself: have you emotional balance, or does your heart guide your life without enough help from your brain? Your answers do not indicate whether or not you have the common sense which holds good qualities from overdoing. For you have heaps and piles and mountains of desirable traits. Beneath a completely feminine appearance you hide manly strength and determination. Your husband was (or will be) surprised the first time he ran (or runs) against your insistence that he should (or shall) do what he knew he ought to do and did not like to. Nothing but your great love and slightly tardy tact will save the situation.

You must always be on your guard against domineering over the weaker personalities that flock to you like homeless dogs. It will be a temptation to hold on to your children after they have grown up. Learn to express your generous love through letting people make their own mistakes, and do not come into the matter till they appeal to you to have their hurts kissed away with understanding and admiration.